Eat it Up!

Lip-smacking recipes for kids

Recipes by Elisabeth de Mariaffi

Illustrations by Jay Stephens,
Steven Charles Manale, Gabriel Morrissette,
Brooke Kerrigan and Wendy Ding

Owl
kids

Contents

Arf
The neighborhood dog

Chick
Dee's best friend

Dee
Chick's best friend

Fang
The bully

Bruno
The friendly monster

Jack
The other bully

Petal
The monkey pal

Robin
Chick's big sister

Shelldon
Dee's little brother

55+ HEALTHY RECIPES

Allergy Info Legend

= no peanuts

= no tree nuts

= **no wheat**

= no dairy

= no eggs

Let's Stay Safe

Cooking is tons of fun, but it can be dangerous. Read these important tips before you begin in the kitchen.

Ask an adult for permission and help

It's fun to cook together and it takes less time.

Wash up

Clean your hands before you begin so germs don't get into the food. Always wash your hands and the cutting board after handling raw meat, fish or eggs. These uncooked foods have germs that could make you sick.

Using sharp tools

- Ask an adult to cut hard food, like raw carrots.

- Always use one hand to hold the food you are cutting and the other to hold the knife.

stop!

- Grate food slowly and carefully. Stop when your hand gets too close to the grater.

- Never put your hand into a blender or food processor, even if it is turned off. Either pour it out or use a large spoon or spatula to get food out.

Using the stove or oven

- Wear fitted clothes and tie back long hair. Loose clothes may accidentally touch a hot element or gas flame and catch fire.

- Wear an apron to protect yourself from hot, splattering food. Heat oil or butter over medium heat so it doesn't splatter.

- An adult should be there to help you slide in or remove food from the oven. Always wear oven mitts.

- When you open a hot oven, stand back a bit to let the heat come out first.

- Turn the handle of your pan toward the back of the stove so it doesn't get knocked off by accident.

- Never touch a stove element because it stays hot for a while after it's turned off.

Let's Get Equipped
Get these gadgets and rule the kitchen!

Cutting board

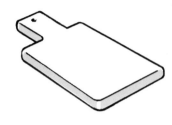

Apron

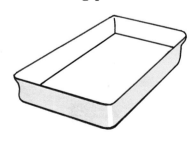

Blender or food processor

Colander

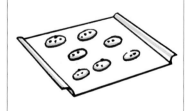

Electric mixer

Baking or casserole dish

Box grater

Cookie cutters

Frying pans

Baking pan

Bundt pan

Cookie sheet

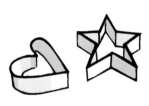

Knives (dinner knives to spread, sharp ones to cut)

Ladle

Oven mitts

Ramekins

Sifter

Measuring cups

Parchment paper

Rolling pin

Spatula

Measuring spoons

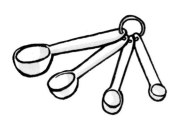

Pasta pot

Saucepans

Vegetable peeler

Mixing bowls

Pitcher

Serving bowl

Whisk

Muffin pan

Pizza cutter

Sieve

Wooden mixing spoon

Let's Get Cooking
Top terms for champ chefs

Bake foods in a hot oven

Batter is a liquid mixture that is cooked until solid

Beat an egg with a fork or whisk

Bite-sized pieces should fit easily in your mouth

Blend food together in a blender or food processor

Boil means to cook a liquid on high heat until it bubbles, or to cook something in very hot water

Brown meat in a pan to cook away any pink color

Chop food into pieces with a knife

Coat food by dipping it fully into batter, liquids or spices

Cook means to heat food to prepare it

Cool baked goods on a rack until they can be touched

Drain to remove liquid from around food, such as water from pasta

Fry foods in hot oil on a stove

Grate cheese or other foods into tiny pieces with a grater or zester

Grease a sheet or pan by rubbing it with butter or oil

Heat foods up using a stove, oven or microwave

Ingredients are the foods and spices used in a recipe

Knead dough by pressing, pushing and pulling it

Lumpy batter is not perfectly smooth

Mash soft foods into a paste with a masher or fork

Measure foods with measuring cups or spoons to find the right amount

Melt solid food like butter or cheese by heating until it turns into a liquid

Mix means to stir together

Pour something from one container into another

Preheat means to heat the oven ahead of time

Purée means to blend soft foods in a blender or food processor until smooth

Sauté foods quickly over high heat with a small amount of oil

Cooking Measurements

Metric		Imperial	
°C	Celsius	°F	Fahrenheit
cm	centimetre	in	inch
g	gram	lb	pound
mL	millilitre	oz	ounce
L	litre	tsp	teaspoon
		tbsp	tablespoon

Scrape batter out of a bowl with a rubber spatula

Serve your cooking to hungry people who want to eat it

Sift dry powders through a sieve to remove lumps

Simmer means to keep liquids just below boiling point

Slice food into thin, even pieces with a knife

Stir ingredients by mixing with a spoon or fork

Thaw means to let frozen food warm up to room temperature

Toss salad items together in a bowl with salad servers

Whisk liquids together to mix them well using a whisk or fork

Clean-up Tips

Cleaning up is part of cooking. If you leave behind a clean kitchen, your parents will let you cook more often!

- Rinse bowls, plates, mixing spoons and other equipment as soon as you're done so the ingredients don't get hard and become difficult to clean.

- Fill a sink with warm, soapy water so you can soak your dirty dishes while you finish cooking.

- Wipe up counters with a damp cloth while you are cooking.

- Put ingredients away as soon as you are done with them.

- Sometimes you can strike a deal with a parent or sibling: they just may agree to wash the dishes if you do the cooking!

Let's Stay Healthy

Your body is like an engine, and food is its fuel. To be at your best, you must eat the right servings, or amounts, of the right foods. Follow this plan every day to help you run, jump, think, laugh and play like a champ!

What's a serving?

A serving is a little different for each food. For example, an apple is one serving of fruit. Ask an adult for help planning your meals.

Every day you should have...

1-2 servings of Meat and Meat Alternatives

This gives your body **protein** to build strong muscles.

2-3 servings of Milk and Milk Alternatives

These contain **calcium**, which builds strong bones and teeth.

4-6 servings of Grains

They give you **energy** — that's your get-up-and-go! Pick breads, pastas and rice made with **whole grains** when you can.

5-6 servings of Fruits and Vegetables

They're packed with **vitamins** and **minerals** that help stop you from getting sick. Remember: fruit juice doesn't count as a serving!

4-6 servings of Water

Water is something your body needs. Try to drink a cup of water every couple of hours.

Remember!

Healthy **fats** and **oils** are yummy brain food! You can find them in olive oil, avocados and fatty fish like salmon. **Skip junk food** like doughnuts, chocolate bars, soft drinks, chips and pastries. These foods will only clog your engine!

Allergy Alert

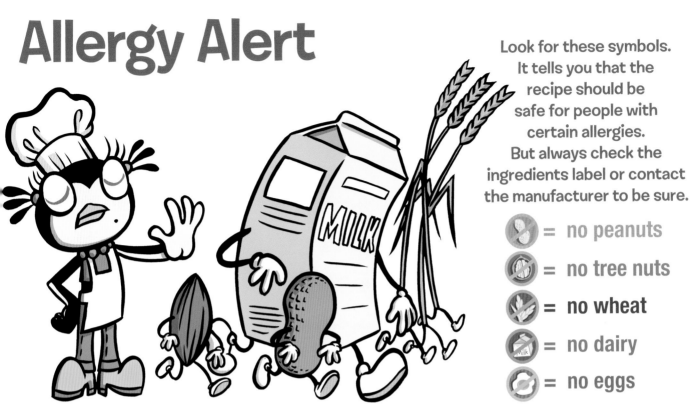

Look for these symbols. It tells you that the recipe should be safe for people with certain allergies. But always check the ingredients label or contact the manufacturer to be sure.

= no peanuts

= no tree nuts

= **no wheat**

= no dairy

= no eggs

Many people have some kind of allergy. Some people are allergic to foods. These are the most common food allergies:

- Peanuts
- Tree nuts (walnuts, almonds, cashews)
- Wheat (wheat-based breads and pastas)
- Dairy (milk, cheese, yogurt, butter)
- Eggs (baked goods, desserts, pancakes)

No laughing matter!

Food allergies can be very serious. Even a tiny bit of the wrong food can cause an awful allergic reaction. Let's say you eat some peanuts with your hands. If you then shake hands with someone who has a peanut allergy, that person can have a really bad reaction! If you have a food allergy, always let others know about it — that way everyone can help make sure you don't get sick.

If you are purchasing packaged, canned or processed ingredients, make sure you check labels to ensure they are allergy-safe.

Delicious alternatives

So how you do prepare meals for someone with a food allergy? For starters, keep that food out of the kitchen! There are also lots of allergy alternatives out there to replace ingredients commonly found in recipes. Here are some easy examples:

- **Instead of milk,** use calcium-fortified soy or rice milk for everything from baking to cereal!

- **Instead of peanut butter,** try almond butter, soy-nut butter or sunflower-seed butter. (Avoid ALL nut butters if you have a tree nut allergy.)

- **Instead of wheat flour,** use flours made from grains like corn, rice, millet, quinoa or buckwheat.

- **Instead of wheat pasta,** use rice, corn, potato or buckwheat pasta.

Buttermilk Power Pancakes
with Yummy Blueberry Sauce

A Dream Breakfast

Wake Up!

It's Breakfast Time

Robin's Marv-ilicious Muffins

Makes: 12 large muffins

Prep: 45 minutes

You'll need:

Dry ingredients:

375 mL (1½ cups) all-purpose flour

250 mL (1 cup) whole wheat flour

175 mL (¾ cup) packed brown sugar

15 mL (1 tbsp) baking powder

2 mL (½ tsp) salt

Wet ingredients:

2 large eggs

250 mL (1 cup) milk

125 mL (½ cup) unsalted butter, melted

1. **Preheat** oven to 200°C (400°F). Line 12 muffin cups with paper liners.

2. **Mix** dry ingredients in large bowl and set aside. In small bowl, **beat** eggs lightly. **Stir** in milk and butter.

Tip **Measuring Trick**
To measure 125 mL (½ cup) of butter, fill a clear, 500 mL (2 cup) measuring cup with 375 mL (1½ cups) of water. Now add small chunks of butter until the water reaches the 500 mL (2 cup) level. The amount of butter you have added equals exactly 125 mL (½ cup). Neat, huh?

3. **Pour** wet ingredients into dry ingredients and stir well. Muffin batter can be **lumpy**.

4. Look at the **You Choose!** box (right) and decide which muffins to make. **Stir** those ingredients into the batter.

5. Spoon batter into muffin cups so they are not quite full. **Bake** for 20 minutes.

6. To check if your muffins are ready, insert a toothpick and make sure it comes out clean. If not, **bake** for 3 more minutes.

7. When muffins are done, place pan on cooling rack. After 10 minutes, slide muffins out of the pan and continue to **cool**.

You Choose!

Pick your favorite muffin, and add the ingredients to your batter at step 4.

Blueberry

7 mL (1½ tsp) grated lemon rind

375 mL (1½ cups) fresh blueberries, *or* frozen blueberries, thawed

Pumpkin-Raisin

250 mL (1 cup) canned pumpkin purée

5 mL (1 tsp) cinnamon

2 mL (½ tsp) ginger

1 mL (¼ tsp) nutmeg

125 mL (½ cup) raisins

Banana-Chocolate Chip

3 ripe bananas, mashed

125 mL (½ cup) chocolate chips

MAKE MY MARV-ILICIOUS MUFFINS *THREE* DIFFERENT WAYS!

Bruno's Breakfast Bake

Makes: 6 servings

Prep: 25 minutes

You'll need:

90 mL (6 tbsp) chopped ham, plus extra for garnish

6 large or extra-large eggs

pinch of salt and pepper

30 mL (2 tbsp) cream

90 mL (6 tbsp) grated cheddar cheese

GRRR!

DON'T WORRY!

THAT'S JUST MY *TUMMY!* I'M A FRIENDLY MONSTER!

1. **Preheat** oven to 180°C (350°F). **Grease** 6 ramekins.

2. Spoon 15 mL (1 tbsp) of ham into each ramekin.

3. Crack 1 egg and **beat** in bowl. Add salt and pepper. **Pour** egg into ramekin. Repeat for other ramekins.

4. Top each with 5 mL (1 tsp) of cream and 15 mL (1 tbsp) of cheese.

5. Place ramekins on cookie sheet. **Bake** for 10 to 12 minutes or until egg sets.

6. Remove cookie sheet with oven mitts. Use mitts to place ramekins on plates. Decorate with ham.

Shelldon's Eggeritos

Makes: 6 servings

Prep: 15 minutes

You'll need:

8 large eggs

45 mL (3 tbsp) milk

pinch of salt and pepper

10 mL (2 tsp) butter

84 g (3 oz) medium cheddar cheese, cubed

3 large whole wheat tortillas (check that it's allergy-safe!)

Make it zesty!

15 mL (1 tbsp) salsa, mild or hot (check that it's allergy-safe!)

CHUCK!

HI-YO EGGERITO!

1. Crack eggs into medium bowl. Add milk and **whisk** together. Add salt and pepper.

2. Melt butter in pan at medium-low until foamy. Add eggs. When they start to cook, add cheese and **stir** until done. Remove from heat.

3. Cut each tortilla in half. Place a scoop of eggs on each half, leaving space around the edges. Add salsa if you wish. Fold bottom up, then fold one side over the other. Secure with toothpick.

Sweet Strawberries and Oranges in
Heavenly Honey Cream

ME FIRST!

OOO!

YUM!

Makes: 4 servings

Prep: 10 minutes

You'll need:

45 mL (3 tbsp) cream

15 mL (1 tbsp) liquid honey

500 mL (2 cups) strawberries, washed and cut into bite-sized pieces

1 large seedless orange, peeled and cut into bite-sized pieces

1. **Whisk** cream and honey together in small bowl until completely blended.

wssk
wssk

2. **Mix** strawberries and oranges together in large bowl. **Pour** honey cream over fruit and **stir**. **Serve** right away or refrigerate. Stir again before serving.

Smilin' Smoothies

SLURP!

SLOOP!

Makes: 2 smoothies

Prep: 5 minutes

You'll need:

Base ingredients:

250 mL (1 cup) plain yogurt

125 mL (½ cup) orange juice

15 mL (1 tbsp) honey

Pick your fruit!

Mighty Mango
250 mL (1 cup) mango chunks, frozen

Superb Strawberry-Banana
250 mL (1 cup) banana slices, frozen
125 mL (½ cup) strawberries, frozen

1. Put the base ingredients and fruit in blender or food processor and **blend** until smooth. If it's too thick, add a little milk and blend again.

(Tip) **Store Frozen Fruit**
Keep fruit in the freezer so you'll always be ready to make a smoothie! If you don't have frozen fruit, blend fresh fruit chunks with three or four ice cubes. It might be noisy, so plug your ears!

Buttermilk Power Pancakes

Makes: 12 to 16 pancakes

Prep: 25 minutes

You'll need:

Dry ingredients:

250 mL (1 cup)
whole wheat flour

250 mL (1 cup)
all-purpose flour

125 mL (½ cup) wheat germ

5 mL (1 tsp) baking soda

15 mL (1 tbsp) brown sugar

5 mL (1 tsp) salt

Wet ingredients:

2 large eggs

500 to 625 mL
(2 to 2½ cups) buttermilk

30 mL (2 tbsp)
butter, melted

Make it sticky!

Serve with maple syrup or
Yummy Blueberry Sauce

1. **Stir** all dry ingredients together in large mixing bowl.

2. In small bowl, **beat** eggs. **Stir** in the buttermilk.

3. Add wet ingredients to dry ingredients and stir. **Stir** in butter. Don't worry if the mixture is **lumpy**.

ARF TURNED **BLUE** BECAUSE HE EATS SO **MUCH** OF THIS **SAUCE!**

Yummy Blueberry Sauce

Makes: about 2 cups
Prep: 10 minutes
You'll need:
375 mL (1½ cups) frozen blueberries, thawed
125 mL (½ cup) maple syrup
15 mL (1 tbsp) lemon juice
15 mL (1 tbsp) cornstarch

4. **Heat** pan to medium-high. Ladle 1 or 2 pancakes into the pan.

spizzle

5. When edges look dry and bubbles appear on top, flip pancakes over and cook for another minute or so. Repeat until batter is gone.

1. **Mix** all ingredients in medium saucepan.

2. Bring to a **boil** over medium heat, stirring occasionally. Lower heat and let **simmer** for 2 minutes.

3. Remove from heat. **Serve** warm.

Homemade Pizza

The Robin Special

WHO WANTS ONE OF MY FABULOUS SANDWICHES?

ME!

I DO!

EAZY COOKING

MIX MIX MIX

SHAKE!

GLUG! GLUG! GLUG!

BLEND... BLEND...

SIZZLE

CHOP! CHOP! CHOP!

Snack Attack

For lunchin' or for munchin'!

Fang's Stuff 'Em Up Sandwiches

DO NOT ENTER!

NO TRESPASSING!

STOP!

DON'T TAKE MY SANDWICHES! THEY'RE **ALL** FOR ME!

Makes:
8 snacks or
4 meals

Prep: 15 minutes

You'll need:

2 eggs

60 mL (¼ cup) milk

1 loaf egg bread, unsliced

butter or margarine

Choose a filling!

• nut butter, honey, banana
  slices and jam

• ham and cheese

• tomato and cheddar

1. Crack eggs into wide, shallow bowl and **beat** gently. Add milk and **stir**. Set aside.

2. Ask an adult to cut 4 slices of egg bread, about 5 cm (2 in) thick. Cut each slice into 2 triangles. Then, in each triangle, cut a horizontal slit almost to the crust.

3. Stuff triangles with your favorite fillings.

4. **Heat** large frying pan on medium-low. Add 10 mL (2 tsp) of butter. Dip each sandwich in egg mixture to **coat** both sides.

5. Add a few sandwiches to pan and press with spatula. **Cook** for 3 minutes per side, until golden brown. Remove from pan.

6. Add 10 mL (2 tsp) of butter to pan and **cook** remaining sandwiches. Let them **cool** because the filling will be piping hot!

Jack's Roll-Around Tuna Grab

I'M JUST BATTY FOR THESE!

Makes: 4 sandwiches

Prep: 15 minutes

You'll need:

2 cans water-packed tuna

60 mL (¼ cup) mayonnaise

30 mL (2 tbsp) minced celery

2 large whole wheat tortillas
(check that it's allergy-safe!)

Spice it up!

- 15 mL (1 tbsp) relish

- 15 mL (1 tbsp)
  minced red onion

- 30 mL (2 tbsp)
  grated cheese

- 15 mL (1 tbsp) salsa
  (check that it's allergy-safe!)

1. **Drain** and rinse tuna. Put in mixing bowl. Add celery, mayonnaise and any optional ingredients. **Mash** together with fork.

2. Soften tortillas in microwave by heating on high for 10 seconds. Divide filling in half and place in middle of each tortilla. Fold ends over filling. Roll tightly, cut in half and serve.

Bouncin'
Black Bean Dip

Makes: 1 bowl of dip

Prep: 15 minutes

You'll need:

540 mL (19 oz) can of black beans

½ medium onion, chopped

1 clove garlic, finely chopped

125 mL (½ cup) salsa (check that it's allergy-safe!)

2 mL (½ tsp) ground cumin

salt and pepper

For dipping:

1 big bag of tortilla chips (check that it's allergy-safe!)

Make it tangy!
15 mL (1 tbsp) lime juice

1. Put about half the beans and all the chopped onion and garlic into a blender. **Blend** until smooth.

2. **Pour** into a bowl. Add the rest of the beans and the salsa and **mix** together with a fork.

3. Add the cumin, a few shakes of salt and pepper, and **stir**.

Skyscraper Sandwich

I COULD EAT **THREE** OF THESE!

Makes:
1 large sandwich –
enough for 2 kids
or 1 grown-up!

Prep: 10 minutes

You'll need:

3 slices whole wheat
or multi-grain bread

butter or mustard

sliced cold cuts such
as ham, Italian salami
or prosciutto

sliced cheese

sliced pickles

mayonnaise

sliced turkey breast

sliced tomatoes
and lettuce

1. On a slice of bread, spread butter or mustard. Layer cold cuts, cheese and pickle slices on this slice.

2. Spread a second slice of bread with mayonnaise and place on first slice. Now top second slice of bread with turkey. Add tomato and lettuce.

3. Add last slice of bread to make three layers. Cut sandwich into 2 triangles and spear each triangle with a fancy toothpick.

Tip **Make a Toasted Melt**
Follow the steps above, but toast the bread and replace the lettuce with more tomato. Wrap the sandwich in aluminum foil and put in the oven at 180° C (350° F) for 5 minutes.

You Choose!

Wanna build a wacky sandwich? Try some of these ingredients:

- tuna salad
- sliced hard-boiled eggs
- mayonnaise
- ketchup
- sliced cheese
- pastrami
- turkey
- cream cheese
- avocado
- potato chips
- raisins
- peanut butter
- hot salsa
- chicken fingers
- chocolate syrup
- jam
- tiny pickles
- grated carrots
- lettuce
- banana slices
- bacon
- salami
- fish sticks

What crazy ingredients would you add to your wacky sandwich?

Chick and Dee's Handful of Scrumptious Snacks

Car Trip Crunch

Makes: about 1.5 L (6 cups)	
Prep: 1 hour	
You'll need:	
250 mL (1 cup) salted, mixed nuts	
375 mL (1½ cups) small pretzels	
1 L (4 cups) mixed dry cereals (try a mix of your favorites)	
60 mL (¼ cup) butter	
1 mL (¼ tsp) garlic salt	
1 mL (¼ tsp) onion salt	
10 mL (2 tsp) Worcestershire sauce	
5 mL (1 tsp) lemon juice	

1. **Preheat** oven to 120°C (250°F). Line a rimmed cookie sheet with parchment paper. **Stir** nuts, pretzels and cereals in the pan.

2. **Melt** butter in saucepan and **stir** in rest of ingredients. Drizzle over cereal and nuts, and stir to coat evenly.

3. **Bake** for 45 minutes, **stirring** every 15 minutes. Store in sealed container for up to 2 months.

> **Tip** Make it nut-free!
> Replace nuts with salted soy nuts or mini-crackers.

Pop 'Em! Pizza Popcorn

Makes: about 2 L (8 cups)

Prep: 10 minutes

You'll need:

60 mL (¼ cup) grated Parmesan cheese

5 mL (1 tsp) garlic powder

5 mL (1 tsp) Italian herb seasoning

5 mL (1 tsp) paprika

2 mL (½ tsp) salt (if using microwave popcorn, do not add salt)

pepper to taste

2 L (8 cups) fresh popcorn (either air-popped or plain microwave popcorn)

30 to 45 mL (2 to 3 tbsp) butter, melted

1. **Stir** Parmesan cheese, garlic powder, Italian seasoning, paprika, salt and pepper together in large bowl.

2. **Toss** popcorn with melted butter. Add seasoning and **mix** well, until popcorn is evenly coated.

Bird Seed

Mix together one of these combos:

- salted, roasted sunflower seeds and raisins

- roasted peanuts and raisins (also known as **GORP**, for Good Old Raisins and Peanuts)

- roasted peanuts or cashews, dried apricots and roasted pumpkin seeds

- dried apples, roasted pumpkin seeds, roasted cashews and raisins

Homemade Pizza

OOF!

MAYBE I PUT ON **TOO MUCH** *CHEESE!*

Dynamite Dough

Makes: dough for 1 pizza	

Prep: 20 minutes (plus 1 hour for dough to rise)

You'll need:

500 mL (2 cups) flour
8 g (¼ oz) instant dried yeast
5 mL (1 tsp) sugar
2 mL (½ tsp) salt
15 mL (1 tbsp) olive oil
250 mL (1 cup) warm water

1. Sift the flour, yeast, sugar and salt together in a large bowl. **Stir** in the oil, then slowly add the water to make a soft dough. You might not need all of the water, so add only a little at a time!

2. Lightly flour your hands and work surface. **Knead** the dough for about 10 minutes, until it becomes smooth and stretchy.

3. Roll the dough into a big ball. Lightly **grease** a large bowl and put the dough inside. Cover the bowl and put the dough in a warm place so it can rise. After about an hour, it will be twice the size! Now you're ready to roll.

Party Pizza

Makes: 4 servings

Prep: 40 minutes

You'll need:

Dynamite Dough
flour for dusting
1 jar pizza sauce (check that it is allergy-safe!) or Rockin' Red Tomato Sauce or Presto Pesto! (pages 86–87)
400 g (14 oz) grated mozzarella cheese

Pick your toppings!

- pepperoni
- sliced red or green pepper
- sliced mushrooms
- tomatoes
- bacon
- ham
- chopped spinach
- chopped broccoli
- pineapple
- feta or ricotta cheese
- sliced red onion
- fresh basil leaves

1. Preheat oven to 230°C (450°F).

2. Sprinkle some flour on a clean, flat surface. Using a rolling pin, roll out the dough into a large, flat circle and place it on the pizza pan.

3. Spread an even layer of sauce on the dough.

4. Top with an even mix of favorite toppings. Don't overload the pizza with too many toppings — everything will cook better that way.

5. Finally, top with an even layer of mozzarella cheese.

6. Bake for 15 to 20 minutes, or until the crust is golden. **Slice** it up and get it while it's hot!

Crunchy Fish Sticks,
Freaky Fries and Sail the Seven Peas

Everybody's a Critic

WELCOME TO *CHEZ CHICK!* I WILL BE YOUR MAÎTRE DEE FOR THE EVENING.

I, SHELLDON, THE FAMOUS FOOD CRITIC, DEMAND PASTA BAKE!

OUI, SIR.

Treat your family and...
Make a Meal!

RECIPES

Sporty Stir-fry Dinner

MENU

Mountain of Veggies Stir-fry

Co-co-coconut Rice

Makes: dinner for 4

Here's the plan:

1. Start cooking the rice.

2. Make your stir-fry sauce.

3. Stir-fry tofu and veggies.

Co-co-coconut Rice

Prep: 50 minutes

You'll need:

500 mL (2 cups) brown rice
398 mL (13.5 oz) can coconut milk
600 mL (2 ⅓ cups) water
1 pinch salt
5 mL (1 tsp) sugar

1. Put everything in a large pot over high heat. Watch closely for it to **boil**.

2. Once boiling, immediately lower the heat, cover the pot and **simmer**.

3. Every 10 minutes or so, **stir** the whole pot a few times and check to make sure the rice isn't sticking to the bottom.

4. After about 40 minutes (for brown rice, white rice takes 15 to 20 minutes), the rice will be tender and ready to eat.

Tip **No Coconut Milk?**
No problem! This recipe works just as well without the coconut milk. Just use 1 L (4 cups) of water instead.

Chopstick How-To
Learn how to eat with chopsticks!

1. Hold the bottom chopstick between the bottom of your thumb and the tip of your ring finger.

2. Hold the top chopstick between your index finger and thumb, and move it up and down to pick up food.

Mountain of Veggies Stir-fry

Prep: 35 minutes

You'll need:

15 mL (1 tbsp) canola oil

1 clove garlic, minced

1 block firm tofu, cut into 2.5 cm (1 inch) cubes

500 mL (2 cups) of your favorite veggies, chopped

For the sauce:

30 mL (2 tbsp) soy sauce

15 mL (1 tbsp) rice vinegar

250 mL (1 cup) vegetable broth (check that it's allergy-safe!)

Make it spicy!

2.5 cm (1 inch) ginger root, peeled and minced

1. Place a large frying pan or wok on the stove over medium heat.

2. Heat the oil in the frying pan briefly, then add the garlic and, if desired, ginger and **fry** for about 30 seconds.

careful, Hot!

3. Turn up the heat to high. **Fry** and **stir** the tofu until lightly browned on all sides. Remove the tofu and set aside.

4. Add the veggies to the pan (add a little more oil to the pan if you need to). Start with the firmer veggies, such as broccoli and carrot, then add the rest a couple of minutes later. **Stir** constantly around the pan and **fry** for about 5 minutes.

5. Pour the soy sauce, rice vinegar and broth into a small bowl and **mix** well. **Stir** this sauce into the stir-fry. Put the tofu back into the pan and let the whole thing stir-fry for another minute. **Serve** immediately on the Co-co-coconut Rice.

You Choose!

All kinds of veggies will work in this dish. Use 500 mL (2 cups) of your favorites, including:

- broccoli florets
- mushrooms
- bell peppers
- baby corn cobs
- carrots
- tomatoes

What else do YOU like in your stir-fry?

The Pirate's Crunch

MENU

Crunchy Fish Sticks

Freaky Fries

Sail the Seven Peas

Makes: dinner for 4

Here's the plan:

1. Cut, season and bake fries.

2. Coat fish with breadcrumbs while fries bake, then add to the oven.

3. Heat peas while everything finishes baking.

Freaky Fries

Prep: 45 minutes	
You'll need:	
250 mL (1 cup) carrots, peeled	
250 mL (1 cup) sweet potatoes, peeled	
250 mL (1 cup) potatoes, peeled	
olive oil	
salt and pepper	

1. **Preheat** oven to 220°C (425°F). Lightly **grease** a large cookie sheet with nonstick cooking spray.

2. Carefully cut the veggies into fries. To do this with potatoes, **slice** them lengthwise, then stack some slices and cut them into fries. The thinner the fries, the crispier they'll be when baked!

3. Place fries in a large mixing bowl. Add olive oil, salt and pepper and **mix** it all together with your hands.

4. Spread the fries on the sheet in a single layer. **Bake** them for 12 to 15 minutes.

5. Carefully take the fries out of the oven and flip them over. Put them back in and **bake** for 10 more minutes, or until nicely browned. Make sure everyone gets all three types of fries!

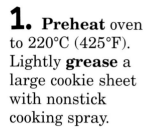

Celery Boat How-To

Learn how to make a celery boat!

1. Cut a piece of celery a little longer than your middle finger.

2. Take a carrot and peel off two long strips. Use scissors to trim the top of each strip into a point.

3. Grab a toothpick. Poke one end into the bottom of a carrot strip. Then poke the other end into the top of the carrot strip to make a sail. Repeat with another toothpick and stick both sails into your celery boat. Bon voyage!

Crunchy Fish Sticks

Prep: 25 minutes

You'll need:

1 egg, lightly beaten

250 mL (1 cup) breadcrumbs
(check that it's allergy-safe!)

salt and pepper

454 g (1 lb) of whitefish
fillet(s), such as sole, halibut,
cod or haddock, cut into strips

1 lemon

ketchup or tartar sauce
for serving (check that it's
allergy-safe!)

Make it spicy!

5 mL (1 tsp) paprika or
chili powder

1. **Preheat** oven to 220°C (425°F). Lightly **grease** a large cookie sheet with nonstick cooking spray.

2. **Beat** the egg in a bowl. Place the breadcrumbs in another bowl. Season with salt and pepper. Add paprika or chili powder, if you wish.

Tip **Try with Chicken!**
In the mood for chicken strips? Just use 454 g (1 lb) of chicken instead of fish. Cut chicken into strips and follow the simple steps.

3. **Coat** a fish strip with the egg mix. Roll the strip in the breadcrumbs so that it's covered. Place the finished stick on the cookie sheet and repeat until all pieces are coated. If you run out of breadcrumbs, just add more to the bowl.

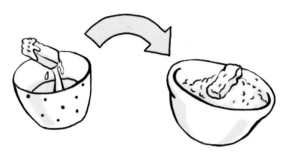

4. **Bake** fish in the oven for 10 to 12 minutes, or until crispy. Flip the fish halfway through. If you're making the whole meal, add the fish to the oven when you flip the fries.

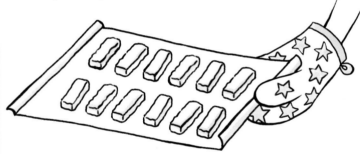

5. **Cut** your lemon into 4 wedges and give everyone a wedge to squeeze on their crunchy fish. **Serve** with tartar sauce or ketchup. Mmmm!

Sail the Seven Peas

Prep: 10 minutes

You'll need:

500 mL (2 cups) peas,
fresh or frozen

15 mL (1 tbsp) olive oil
or butter

salt and pepper

1. Fill a medium-sized saucepan with salted water. Bring to a **boil**. Add peas and **cook** for 5 minutes.

2. With a grown-up's help, **drain** the peas into a colander and then put back into the pot. Add the olive oil, salt and pepper and **stir**.

Winter Warmer
Sweet and
Spicy Dinner

Meaty Mini-Pies

Makes: about 12 small meat pies (you could also make 1 large pie and slice it)

Prep: 30 minutes

Baking time: 25 to 35 minutes

You'll need:

2 packages frozen tart shells (or 2 frozen large pie shells)

60 mL (¼ cup) raisins

30 mL (2 tbsp) chopped dried apricots

15 mL (1 tbsp) vegetable oil

½ cooking onion, chopped

2 mL (½ tsp) ground cinnamon

0.5 mL (⅛ tsp) ground cloves

227 g (½ lb) lean ground beef

2 mL (½ tsp) salt

1 mL (¼ tsp) pepper

1 egg

1. **Mix** raisins and apricots in small bowl and cover with warm water. Set aside until ready to use.

2. In large pan, **heat** oil over medium-low heat. Add onion and cook 5 minutes or until soft. **Stir** in cinnamon and cloves.

3. Add beef and turn up heat to medium. Break up meat with the back of a spoon. Add salt and pepper and stir. **Brown** for 5 to 10 minutes.

4. **Drain** dried fruit. Add fruit to meat mixture and **stir**. Turn off heat and let **cool**.

drip drip

5. Spoon 60 mL (¼ cup) of filling into each tart shell. **Beat** egg in a small bowl. Use a pastry brush to brush a little egg around the edge of each filled pie.

6. To make the tops, remove remaining tart shells from foil cups. Flip upside down on top of each pie and press down gently with your palm. Use your thumb to press the edges together.

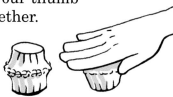

7. Gently poke the tops with a fork to make tiny holes for steam to escape. Brush tops with beaten egg.

8. **Preheat** oven to 190°C (375°F). Place mini-pies on a baking sheet. **Bake** for 20 to 25 minutes, or until golden brown. Let **cool**. If you are making a large single pie, bake for 45 to 50 minutes.

Tip — Short on Time?

If you don't have time to make the Meaty Mini-Pies all at once, make the filling one day and then fill and bake the pies the next.

Hurry Curry Pumpkin Soup

Prep: 15 minutes

You'll need:

250 mL (1 cup) canned pumpkin purée

625 mL (2 ½ cups) beef or vegetable broth

15 mL (1 tbsp) honey

1 mL (¼ tsp) black pepper

5 mL (1 tsp) salt (no salt if using canned broth)

1 mL (¼ tsp) curry powder

250 mL (1 cup) light cream or milk

Make it crunchy!
handful of seasoned croutons

1. **Whisk** together all ingredients except cream or milk in large saucepan. Bring to a **boil**, then turn heat to low. Let soup **cook** for about 5 minutes.

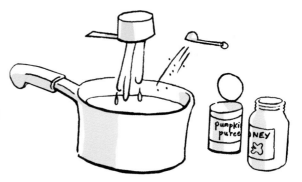

2. Turn heat off and **whisk** in cream or milk. Ladle soup into bowls.

3. Float some croutons on top of each bowl before serving, if you wish.

MENU

Better Be Butter Chicken

Mmmmango Lassi

A Pillow of Rice and Peas

Makes: dinner for 4

Here's the plan:

1. Cook the butter chicken.

2. Make the Mmmmango Lassi and put in fridge.

3. Cook the rice and peas while the chicken bakes.

Sloppy Supper

Better Be Butter Chicken

Prep: 90 minutes

You'll need:

125 mL (½ cup) tandoori or tikka curry paste (check that it is allergy-safe!)
414 mL (14 oz) can crushed tomatoes
250 mL (1 cup) plain yogurt
salt and pepper
3 boneless, skinless chicken breasts
45 mL (3 tbsp) butter
1 onion, thinly sliced
60 mL (4 tbsp) heavy cream

1. Preheat the oven to 180°C (350°F). **Mix** the curry paste, crushed tomatoes, yogurt, and a few shakes of salt and pepper together in a big bowl. This is the sauce.

2. Cut the chicken into **bite-sized** chunks. Add them to the sauce and **stir** together.

3. Put a large ovenproof frying pan on the stove over medium-low heat. Gently **melt** the butter in the pan.

4. Fry the onions slowly in the butter until nice and soft.

5. Add the chicken and sauce to the onions and **stir**. Turn up the heat and bring to a gentle **boil**.

6. Stir in the cream. Carefully put the pan in the oven and **bake** for 1 hour.

7. Remove from the oven using oven mitts and let sit for 5 minutes.

Tip **Extra-yummy Chicken!** Combine the chicken chunks and sauce together the night before and put it in the fridge. This is called marinating.

Mmmmango Lassi

Prep: 10 minutes

You'll need:

2 ripe mangoes
500 mL (2 cups) plain or vanilla yogurt
250 mL (1 cup) milk
15 mL (1 tbsp) honey

1. Have an adult peel and roughly **chop** the mangoes.

2. **Mix** all ingredients in a blender on high until smooth and creamy.

3. **Pour** in a pitcher and let cool in the fridge until dinner is ready.

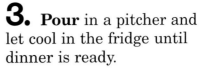

WRRRR

A Pillow of Rice and Peas

Prep: 30 minutes

You'll need:

500 mL (2 cups) basmati rice or rice of your choice
750 mL (3 cups) water
15 mL (1 tbsp) olive oil
salt
375 mL (1 ½ cups) peas, frozen or fresh

1. **Pour** the rice, water, oil and a few shakes of salt into a pot. Put the lid on and bring to a **boil**.

2. When it boils, turn down the heat to low and **simmer** for 15 to 20 minutes. Stir occasionally to be sure the rice isn't sticking to the pot.

3. When the rice is finished, add the peas and **stir** them in — the heat from the rice will **cook** the peas perfectly! Turn off the heat and put the lid back on until the butter chicken is ready.

Yummy Tummy
Pasta Meal

MENU

Ooey-Gooey Pasta

Shelldon's Spinach Salad

Drippy Dressing

Makes: dinner for 4

Here's the plan:

1. Pick and prepare your pasta fillings.

2. Cook the pasta. Add sauce and bake.

3. Make salad while the pasta is baking.

MUNCH MUNCH

Ooey-Gooey Pasta

Prep: 60 minutes

You'll need:

750 mL (3 cups) of medium dry pasta, such as penne, rigatoni, farfalle or fusilli

olive oil or butter

1 jar pasta sauce (check that it is allergy-safe!) or Rockin' Red Tomato Sauce (page 86)

For the filling:

227 g (½ lb) ground beef, turkey or pork

250 mL (1 cup) mushrooms, sliced

250 mL (1 cup) broccoli florets, chopped

1 red pepper, chopped

500 mL (2 cups) grated cheddar or mozzarella cheese

For the topping:

125 mL (½ cup) grated Parmesan cheese

Tip Favorite Fillings
Feel free to replace the veggies in your pasta with 1 or 2 cups of your own favorite fillings!

1. **Preheat** the oven to 190°C (375°F). **Grease** a large 10 cm (4 in) deep baking dish with some olive oil or melted butter.

2. **Heat** a large pan over medium heat. Add the ground meat and mushrooms and **fry** until browned. **Drain** the pan and set it aside until later.

sizzle

3. Fill a large pasta pot with salted water and bring to a **boil**. **Cook** pasta as directed on the package.

Bubble bubble

4. When the pasta is done, get a grown-up to **drain** it into a colander over the sink.

drip! drip!

5. Turn off the heat, **pour** a little olive oil in the pot, put the pasta back and **stir**. Add most of the sauce and all of your fillings to the pot. **Stir** so that everything is nicely mixed.

6. Add the pasta mixture to your baking dish. Top everything with the rest of your sauce and then a layer of Parmesan cheese. **Bake** in the oven for 30 minutes, until the cheese is golden and delicious.

Shelldon's Spinach Salad

Prep: 15 minutes
You'll need:
150 g (5 oz) washed baby spinach or lettuce
2 ripe tomatoes or 1 red pepper
1 cucumber
1 carrot, peeled

1. Place spinach into a large salad bowl. Replace with lettuce if you wish.

2. Wash the vegetables. **Chop** the tomatoes or red pepper into wedges. **Slice** about 8 cm (3 in) of a cucumber. Add the vegetables to the spinach.

3. Carefully **grate** the carrot and set aside.

4. Make Drippy Dressing and add to the salad just before serving. Top each salad bowl with a little pile of grated carrot. Mmmm!

Drippy Dressing

Prep: 10 minutes
You'll need:
45 mL (3 tbsp) olive oil
15 mL (1 tbsp) balsamic vinegar
2 mL (½ tsp) Dijon or other sharp mustard
salt and pepper

1. **Pour** the oil, vinegar and mustard into a bowl and **whisk** with a fork.

2. Add 5 shakes of salt and 2 shakes of pepper.

3. When it's time to eat, add most of the dressing to the salad and **toss**. Remember to **whisk** the dressing before pouring.

Totally Terrific Tacos

The Missing Munchies

WOW! LOTS OF GUESTS!

COOL TUNES!

AWESOME DECORATIONS!

Party Time!

Fun to make, fun to eat and fun to share

RECIPES

Tobogganing Picnic

Melty Munchies

Makes: 4 sandwiches	
Prep: 20 minutes	
You'll need:	
1 loaf of whole-grain bread	
mustard	
8 slices ham	
4 slices Swiss or your favorite cheese	
butter	

1. Spread a little mustard on 2 slices of bread.

2. Place 2 ham slice and 1 slice of cheese on a slice of bread.

3. Close the sandwich and lightly butter the outside. Repeat steps for 3 more sandwiches.

4. **Heat** a frying pan over medium heat. **Fry** each sandwich until golden brown on both sides, pressing down with a spatula to flatten. Repeat until all sandwiches are done.

5. **Serve** right away or wrap in foil and pack for your picnic.

sizzle

Tobogganing Picnic continued . . . ▶

Creamy Mashed Potato Soup

Makes:	8 cups
Prep:	1 hour

You'll need:

2 leeks
1 kg (2 lb) peeled potatoes (4 large)
30 mL (2 tbsp) butter
1.5 L (6 cups) water
5 mL (1 tsp) salt
1 mL (¼ tsp) pepper
175 mL (¾ cup) 10% cream

1. Remove the hard outer leaves from the leeks. Cut the soft inside leaves in half lengthwise and wash well, rinsing off any dirt. **Chop** potatoes into small chunks.

2. In large pot, **melt** butter over medium-low heat. Add leeks and **stir** well into the butter. **Cook** for 5 minutes, or until soft.

3. Add potatoes and **stir**. Add water, salt and pepper. Bring to a **boil** and then turn to low. Cover and **cook** for about 35 minutes.

4. **Pour** soup into a blender or food processor and **purée** until smooth. Carefully pour it back into the pot. **Stir** in cream. Warm over low heat, but don't boil.

5. **Pour** into a thermos and get ready to hit the hills!

Hot Chocolate

Makes:	6 cups
Prep:	5 minutes

You'll need:

1.25 L (5 cups) milk
160 mL (⅔ cup) cocoa mix from page 88
marshmallows

1. **Heat** milk in a large saucepan over medium-high until it's just beginning to boil. Turn down heat.

2. **Whisk** cocoa mix into hot milk until well mixed. Carefully **pour** mixture into a Thermos. Add marshmallows just before drinking!

Tip **Make it Cold**
Serve this soup ice cold in the summertime! The name for this cold soup is *vichyssoise* (SAY: vee-shee-swaz).

Brown Sugar Shortbread

Makes: about 30 cookies

Prep: 45 minutes

You'll need:

500 mL (2 cups) all-purpose flour

1 mL (¼ tsp) salt

250 mL (1 cup) unsalted butter, softened

125 mL (½ cup) packed brown sugar

5 mL (1 tsp) vanilla

1. **Preheat** oven to 160°C (325°F). Line a cookie sheet with parchment paper.

2. **Stir** flour and salt together in small bowl. Set aside.

3. In large bowl, **beat** butter with electric mixer until light and fluffy.

4. Add sugar and **beat** for 3 minutes. **Scrape** sides of bowl with spatula. Beat in vanilla.

Bzzz

5. Add flour and salt to mixture and **beat** on low until combined. Dough should stick together when squeezed.

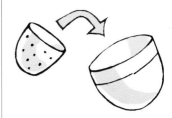

6. Shape dough into small balls and place on cookie sheet, about 4 cm (1½ in) apart. Flatten slightly with a fork.

smoooosh

7. **Bake** 15 to 20 minutes until firm. **Cool** for 10 minutes on cookie sheet. Remove from sheet and continue to cool.

Dee's Sleepover Extravaganza

MENU

Peach Fizz

Get Up and Guacamole

Totally Terrific Taco Buffet

Great Balls of Ice Cream

Breakfast Quesadillas

Serves: 6 sleepers

Peach Fizz

Makes: 6 drinks

Prep: 10 minutes

You'll need:

250 mL (1 cup) coarse red sugar

sparkling peach or peach-apple juice

berry juice or fruit punch

6 fancy glasses

1. **Pour** sugar into small bowl. Put 2 cm (1 in) of water in another bowl.

2. Dip the rim of a glass into the water. Dip wet rim into sugar until it is coated. Put glass on table, right side up, and let dry. Repeat for all 6 glasses.

3. Carefully fill each glass about half full with sparkling peach juice. Add berry juice for color.

Get Up and Guacamole

Makes: about 2 cups

Prep: 10 minutes

You'll need:

2 ripe avocados

1 lime

5 mL (1 tsp) salt

pepper to taste

Spice it up!

- 1 clove garlic, crushed
- 1 ripe tomato, chopped
- 125 mL (½ cup) cilantro leaves, chopped

1. Cut avocados in half and remove pits. Scoop avocado into bowl and **mash**.

2. Cut lime in half and squeeze juice into small bowl. **Pour** juice over avocados and **blend** with salt and pepper. Add garlic, tomato or cilantro, if you wish.

Sleepover continued . . . ▶

Totally Terrific Taco Buffet

Makes: 12 tacos

Prep: 45 minutes

You'll need:

12 taco shells
(check that it's allergy-safe!)

30 mL (2 tbsp) vegetable oil

454 g (1 lb) lean ground beef

1 yellow onion, chopped

5 mL (1 tsp) oregano

5 mL (1 tsp) salt

1 mL (¼ tsp) cumin

1 mL (¼ tsp) pepper

For the fillings:

sour cream

½ head lettuce, shredded

500 mL (2 cups) cheddar
cheese, grated (or buy
pre-grated cheese)

1 jar salsa (check that
it's allergy-safe!)

Get Up and Guacamole
(page 63)

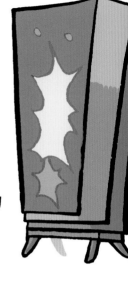

1. Place fillings in separate serving bowls on table.

2. For meat filling, **heat** oil in large saucepan over medium-low. Add onion and **stir**. Cover pan. Stir occasionally with wooden spoon until onions are soft and clear.

3. **Measure** spices in small bowl, then add to onions. Add beef and break up with the back of a spoon.

4. **Brown** for 10 minutes, or until meat has no pink spots. Spoon meat into a large bowl and place on table.

5. Warm taco shells in oven at 150°C (300°F) for about 3 minutes. Now invite all your guests to make their own Totally Terrific Tacos.

Great Balls of Ice Cream

Makes: 6 servings

Prep: 10 minutes

You'll need:

12 gingersnap cookies

vanilla ice cream

1. Place the cookies in a sealed plastic bag. Use your hands or a rolling pin to crush the cookies into tiny crumbs. **Pour** the crumbs into a mixing bowl.

2. Dig out a generous scoop of ice cream and place it in the center of the bowl. Quickly roll the ice cream in the cookie crumbs until well covered. Place in a serving bowl.

3. Repeat until everyone has a Great Ball of Ice Cream. Experiment with your own combos of ice cream and cookie!

Breakfast Quesadillas

Makes: 6 servings

Prep: 30 minutes

You'll need:

1 package of 8 whole wheat or corn tortillas (check that it's allergy-safe!)

2 handfuls of grated cheddar or 8 cheddar slices

4 apples, thinly sliced

ground cinnamon

sugar

Make it sweet!

maple syrup for dipping

1. **Heat** a frying pan on medium-high.

2. Place a tortilla on a plate. Spread some cheese on the tortilla. Place a layer of apple slices on top of the cheese.

3. Sprinkle some cinnamon and sugar over the apples. Top it with another layer of cheddar.

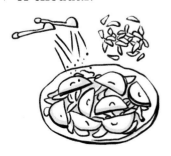

4. Gently slide the tortilla off the plate and into the pan. Top with a second tortilla and **heat** in the pan for 5 minutes, or until lightly browned. (Meanwhile, start building a second quesadilla!)

5. Press the first quesadilla flat with your spatula and flip it over. **Toast** it for another 4 to 5 minutes, or until crispy, then remove.

6. Cut into 6 pieces and **serve** with maple syrup. Start frying the next quesadilla while everyone eats!

Summer Sprinkler Party

MENU

Real Lemonade

Mini Mouthfuls

Fun Fruit Kebabs

Petal Pops

Serves: 8 really hot kids

Real Lemonade

Makes: 750 mL (3 cups) of lemon syrup, or 8 glasses of lemonade

Prep: 20 minutes, plus a few hours to chill

You'll need:

6 lemons

250 mL (1 cup) water

375 mL (1½ cups) sugar

1.25 L (5 cups) cold water

extra-thin slices of lemon to garnish

1. Squeeze lemons to make 375 mL (1½ cups) of juice. Set aside.

2. Stir 250 mL (1 cup) water and sugar in small saucepan. Bring to a **boil** over medium-high heat. Remove from heat and **stir** until sugar is dissolved. Let **cool**.

3. Stir sugar syrup into lemon juice and refrigerate until chilled.

4. Pour lemon syrup into a pitcher. Add the cold water. Decorate glasses with lemon slices.

yum!

Tip **Fizzy Lemonade**
For some bubbly fun, use soda water instead of plain water.

Mini Mouthfuls

Makes: 16 bites

Prep: 5 minutes

You'll need:

16 cherry or grape tomatoes

16 fresh basil leaves

1 package of mozzarella or bocconcini cheese

16 toothpicks

1. Slide one tomato, one basil leaf and one **bite-sized** piece of cheese onto a toothpick. If the tomato is a little big, cut in half before sticking it on the toothpick.

2. Store in the fridge until ready to eat. Yummy and super-easy!

Fun Fruit Kebabs

Makes: 8 servings

Prep: 10 minutes

You'll need:

8 bamboo skewers

Pick your fruit!

- bananas
- strawberries
- pineapple chunks
- seedless red or green grapes
- apple chunks
- and more…

1. Peel and cut the fruit into **bite-sized** chunks or slices. Carefully slide alternating kinds of fruit onto the skewers.

2. Store in the fridge until ready to eat. You can use different types of fruit on your kebabs if you like.

Petal Pops

Makes: 9 banana pops

Prep: 20 minutes, plus at least 2 hours in the freezer

You'll need:

3 bananas

9 popsicle sticks

500 mL (2 cups) semi-sweet chocolate chips

250 mL (1 cup) sprinkles, chopped nuts, candy sequins or other edible decorations

1. Line a large cookie sheet with waxed paper. Peel bananas and cut each into 3 pieces. Push a stick partway into each chunk and put on cookie sheet. Place in freezer for about an hour, or until frozen.

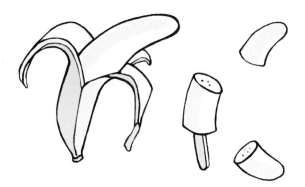

2. **Heat** 4 cm (2 in) of water in a saucepan until boiling. Remove from heat. Place a metal mixing bowl onto rim of saucepan. The bottom of the bowl should be over the water, but not sitting in it. **Pour** chocolate chips into bowl. **Stir** until melted.

3. **Pour** decorations onto a shallow plate. Dip each frozen banana into the melted chocolate. Use the back of a spoon to help **coat** each banana.

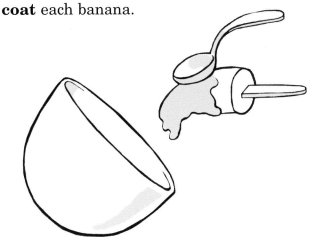

4. Roll each chocolatey banana in decorations. Place back on waxed paper. Put cookie sheet in freezer for 2 hours or overnight.

Swirly Twirly Cinnamunch

The Desserter

DEE! HEY DEE!

WEIRD.

DEE, COME BACK! IT'S TIME TO PLAY BASEBALL!

Save some room for...
DEE-sserts!

RECIPES

Raisin Rounds

Makes: about 24 biscuits

Prep: 1 hour

You'll need:

750 mL (3 cups) all-purpose flour

15 mL (1 tbsp) baking powder

2 mL (½ tsp) baking soda

2 mL (½ tsp) salt

7 mL (1½ tsp) sugar

175 mL (¾ cup) cold, unsalted butter

375 mL (1½ cups) buttermilk

125 mL (½ cup) raisins

You Choose!

Instead of raisins, try one of these:

125 mL (½ cup) grated cheese

125 mL (½ cup) dried cherries and chocolate chips

1. **Preheat** oven to 190°C (375°F). Line 2 cookie sheets with parchment paper.

2. **Measure** flour, baking powder, baking soda, salt and sugar into food processor. **Blend** on low for a minute until combined.

3. Cut butter into small pieces. Add to food processor. **Blend** on medium-low for 5 seconds at a time, until the mixture looks like fat breadcrumbs.

4. **Pour** mixture into large mixing bowl and **stir** in buttermilk. The dough will be sticky. Stir in raisins or **You Choose** (left).

5. Place dough on a floured cutting board and sprinkle a little flour on top. Use your hands to pat dough until it is 1½ cm (½ in) thick.

6. Use a drinking glass or 6 cm (2½ in) round cookie cutter to cut out dough rounds. Place rounds on cookie sheet. Gather dough scraps, pat them again and cut more rounds.

7. Bake rounds for 15 minutes, until slightly golden. **Cool** on cookie sheets for 5 minutes. Transfer to cooling rack.

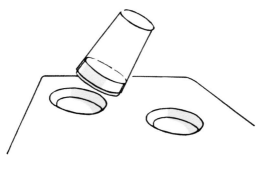

Baked Apples

Ai-yi-yi! IT TASTES LIKE APPLE PIE!

Prep: 10 minutes

Baking time: 45 minutes

You'll need:

6 large washed apples, spy or golden delicious are best

80 mL (1/3 cup) packed brown sugar

5 mL (1 tsp) cinnamon

30 mL (2 tbsp) butter

vanilla ice cream

1. **Preheat** oven to 180°C (350°F).

2. Use apple corer to remove core of each apple. Leave about 3 cm (1 in) of apple core at the bottom so filling doesn't run out. Save the tops.

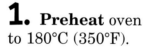

3. Line baking pan with parchment paper or **grease** with butter. Place apples in pan.

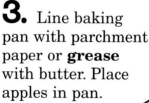

4. **Stir** sugar and cinnamon together. Divide sugar mixture between the 6 apples and fill each hole.

5. Add 5 mL (1 tsp) of butter to each hole. Cover with apple top.

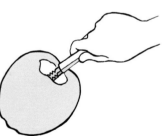

6. **Bake** for 45 minutes. **Serve** warm with vanilla ice cream!

Yogurt Arf-ait

Makes: 4 servings

Prep: 10 minutes

You'll need:

4 seedless mandarin oranges, sliced, or 2 cans mandarin oranges, drained

125 mL (½ cup) chopped almonds

250 mL (1 cup) vanilla yogurt

chocolate syrup

1. Take half of the orange slices and divide them equally between 4 glasses.

2. Add 15 mL (1 tbsp) of almonds to each glass.

3. Add 60 mL (¼ cup) of vanilla yogurt to each glass.

4. Add another layer of orange slices. Top with chocolate syrup and 15 mL (1 tbsp) of almonds. Refrigerate until ready to serve.

You Choose!

Layer these ingredients to make new Arf-ait flavors.

Blueberry Arf-ait
500 mL (2 cups) Yummy Blueberry Sauce (page 21)
125 mL (½ cup) granola
250 mL (1 cup) vanilla yogurt

Banana-Maple Walnut Arf-ait
4 bananas, sliced
125 mL (½ cup) chopped walnuts
250 mL (1 cup) vanilla yogurt
maple syrup for topping

Perfectly Peachy Crisp

Makes: 6 servings

Prep: 15 minutes

Baking time: 35 to 40 minutes

You'll need:

Peach mixture:

2 796 mL (27 oz) cans sliced peaches in juice

80 mL (2 tbsp) flour

75 mL (⅓ cup) brown sugar

Topping:

125 mL (½ cup) all-purpose flour

175 mL (¾ cup) large-flake rolled oats

2 mL (½ tsp) salt

125 mL (½ cup) brown sugar

125 mL (½ cup) unsalted butter

 Try Another Fruit
You could replace the peaches with other fruit, like apples or berries.

1. **Preheat** oven to 180°C (350°F). **Grease** 2 L (8 cup) casserole dish.

2. **Drain** peaches in sieve. In large mixing bowl, **stir** peaches, flour and brown sugar together. Set aside.

3. **Mix** flour, oats and salt in another bowl. Crumble in brown sugar with your fingers to get rid of lumps. **Melt** butter in saucepan. **Pour** over flour mixture. **Stir**.

4. Spoon peaches into casserole dish. Use your hands to crumble topping mixture over fruit. **Bake** for 35 to 40 minutes, until golden and bubbling. **Cool** on rack. **Serve** warm with vanilla ice cream or frozen yogurt.

OPEN WIDE, SHELLDON!

Cups o' Cake

Makes:	12 cupcakes
Prep:	1 hour

You'll need:

175 mL (¾ cup) unsweetened cocoa

250 mL (1 cup) all-purpose flour

5 mL (1 tsp) baking powder

1 mL (¼ tsp) salt

175 mL (¾ cup) unsalted butter, at room temperature

250 mL (1 cup) sugar

2 large eggs

5 mL (1 tsp) vanilla

125 mL (½ cup) milk

1. **Preheat** oven to 180°C (350°F). Line 12 muffin cups with paper liners.

2. **Sift** cocoa, flour, baking powder and salt together. Set aside.

3. In large bowl, **beat** butter and sugar with electric mixer until light and fluffy. Add eggs one at a time, beating well. Beat in vanilla.

SEVEN DOWN, FIVE TO GO!

URP!

EXCUSE ME.

Cool Icing

Mix the icing up while your Cups o' Cake are baking!

Prep: 15 minutes
You'll need:
250 (1 cup) unsalted butter, at room temperature
750 mL (3 cups) icing sugar
60 mL (¼ cup) light cream
food coloring
candy decorations (check that it's allergy-safe!)

1. **Beat** butter with an electric mixer. Add icing sugar slowly until mixture is fluffy. Add cream and beat well.

2. Separate icing into smaller bowls and **beat** different food coloring into each. Keep adding until it's the color you want.

5. Spoon batter into muffin cups. **Bake** for 25 minutes, or until a toothpick inserted into the center of a cupcake comes out clean. **Cool** on rack.

4. Add half the flour mixture and **beat.** Add milk and beat. Add the remaining flour mixture and beat for 3 minutes.

3. Spread icing on cupcakes when they are completely cool. Add candy decorations.

Swirly Twirly
Cinnamunch

VERY STICKY, VERY *YUMMY!*

Makes: one large loaf

Prep: 2 hours and 45 minutes total
work time: 45 minutes
rising time: 1½ hours
baking time: 30 minutes

You'll need:

For the dough:

60 mL (¼ cup) warm water

60 mL (¼ cup plus a pinch) white sugar

1 package dry active yeast

30 mL (2 tbsp) unsalted butter

5 mL (1 tsp) salt

175 mL (¾ cup) warm milk

2 large eggs

875 mL (3½ cups) all-purpose flour

For the coating:

175 mL (¾ cup) packed brown sugar

125 mL (½ cup) chopped walnuts or pecans

10 mL (2 tsp) cinnamon

125 mL (½ cup) unsalted butter

For the icing:

30 mL (2 tbsp) milk

300 mL (1¼ cup) icing sugar

1. **Pour** warm water in small bowl and add pinch of sugar. Sprinkle yeast on top and **stir** gently. Set aside for 10 minutes, or until yeast is dissolved and looks foamy. **Grease** a 25-cm (10-in) Bundt pan and a medium bowl.

2. Put remaining white sugar, butter, salt, warm milk and eggs in a mixing bowl. **Pour** in yeast mixture and **mix** well with dough hooks of an electric mixer or by hand with a wooden spoon.

3. Add flour slowly and **mix** on low speed. Once dough is blended, **knead** with electric mixer for 1 minute or with your hands for 5 minutes.

4. Pat sticky dough into a ball and place in buttered bowl. Turn it over once to **coat** with butter, and then cover with a clean cloth. Set aside for 20 minutes.

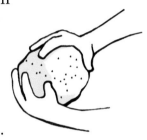

5. **Mix** brown sugar, nuts and cinnamon in a small bowl. **Melt** butter and place in another bowl.

6. After 20 minutes, take dough out of bowl and cut into 4 equal pieces. Roll each piece into a log, and cut each log into 12 pieces. Roll each piece into a ball.

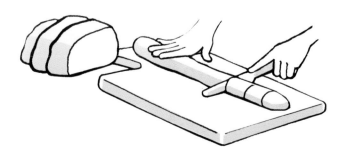

7. Make an assembly line. With one hand, dip a ball into the butter. Then with the other hand, roll it around in the sugar mixture. Stack the balls of dough close together in the buttered Bundt pan.

8. Cover the pan with a clean cloth and set in a warm place to rise for 1 to 1½ hours. It should double in size.

9. **Preheat** oven to 180°C (350°F). **Bake** for 30 minutes, or until golden brown. When done, remove from oven. Let **cool** in pan for about 20 minutes. Then turn upside down on a serving plate. Allow to **cool** completely before icing.

10. **Stir** icing sugar and milk together in small bowl until smooth. Use a spoon to drizzle icing over bread. Let it dribble into center and outside of bread.

Soup in a Jar,
Hot Cider Sacks and
Cocoa and Spoons

Lost and Found

Kitchen Gifts

Unwrap, then eat!

RECIPES

Soup in a Jar

Makes: 1 jar of pasta and pea soup mix

Prep: 10 minutes

You'll need:

125 mL (½ cup) yellow split peas

125 mL (½ cup) small pasta

125 mL (½ cup) red lentils

125 mL (½ cup) pearl barley

30 mL (2 tbsp) dried parsley

30 mL (2 tbsp) dried onion

5 mL (1 tsp) dried thyme

5 mL (1 tsp) dried oregano

Special equipment:

glass pint jar

ribbon

cooking instruction label

1. **Pour** half the split peas in jar. Then layer half the pasta, half the lentils and half the barley. Sprinkle dried parsley around edges. Repeat layering with remaining peas, pasta, lentils and barley. Sprinkle dried onion around edges. Top with thyme and oregano.

2. Close lid tightly and tie with ribbon. Make an instruction label and tie to jar. You can create your own label using these instructions and decorate it.

WHACK!

Soup in a Jar

To: **Winnie Brooke**

From:

Add this soup mix to 2 litres (8 cups) of soup stock or water in a large pot and bring to a boil. Reduce heat to low, cover the pot, and simmer for 50 minutes or until the split peas are tender.

Happy slu...

YUM

(Tip) **Put this on your label!**
Add this soup mix to 2 L (8 cups) of soup stock or water in a large pot and bring to a boil. Reduce heat to low, cover pot and simmer for for 50 minutes, or until the split peas are tender.

Hot Cider Sacks

Makes: 6 sacks

Prep: 15 minutes

You'll need:

6 cinnamon sticks

30 whole cardamom pods

30 whole cloves

18 slices of crystallized ginger, about 3 cm (1¼ in) each

Special equipment:

cheesecloth

kitchen twine

glass pint jar

MY TEACHER IS GOING TO LOVE THESE!

Tip **Put this on your label!**
For mulled cider, simmer 2 L (8 cups) of apple cider with one sack in a covered pot for 30 minutes. Serve in mugs.

1. Cut out six 13 cm (5 in) squares of cheesecloth. Lay them out on a large work surface.

snippity snip

2. Break each cinnamon stick into 3 pieces. Place 3 cinnamon stick pieces, 5 cardamom pods, 5 cloves and 3 pieces of ginger on each square of cheesecloth.

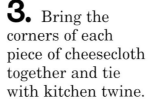

3. Bring the corners of each piece of cheesecloth together and tie with kitchen twine.

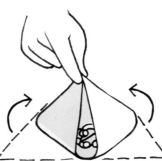

4. Pack the sacks into a jar and attach a label with the instructions above.

So Many Super Sauces!

Rockin' Red Tomato Sauce

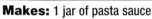

Makes: 1 jar of pasta sauce

Prep: 40 minutes

You'll need:

30 mL (2 tbsp) olive oil

1 onion, chopped

2 garlic cloves, finely chopped

15 mL (1 tbsp) white or red wine vinegar

830 mL (28 oz) can diced or crushed tomatoes

salt and pepper

Make it zesty!

1 handful fresh basil leaves, chopped

Special equipment:

a glass pint jar

1. **Heat** a deep saucepan over medium low heat. **Pour** in and warm the olive oil.

2. **Fry** the onions and garlic for 5 minutes until soft.

3. Add wine vinegar, **stir** and **fry** together for about 30 seconds.

4. Add the can of tomatoes. Bring to a **boil** and **simmer** for 15 minutes.

5. Season the sauce with salt and pepper, and the basil leaves, if you like. **Serve** immediately or let it **cool** and then scoop into a jar.

Presto Pesto!

Makes: 1 small jar of pasta sauce

Prep: 15 minutes

You'll need:

Handful pine nuts

2 large handfuls fresh basil leaves

2 garlic cloves, chopped

60 mL (¼ cup) freshly grated Parmesan cheese

45 mL (3 tbsp) olive oil, plus extra to cover

Special equipment:

a glass half-pint jar

1. Add all of the ingredients to a food processor or blender. **Mix** until well blended into a sticky, gooey paste.

2. Scoop the paste into a jar. Drizzle just enough olive oil to cover the pesto and seal the jar.

 Tip **No heat required!** Pesto is not cooked like other sauces. Instead, add it to freshly cooked pasta and mix well. Try it as a spread on sandwiches, too!

Dreamy Creamy Sauce

Makes: 1 jar of pasta sauce

Prep: 20 minutes

You'll need:

15 mL (1 tbsp) butter

400 mL (1½ cups) heavy cream

125 mL (½ cup) freshly grated Parmesan cheese

salt and pepper

Special equipment:

a glass pint jar

1. **Melt** your butter in a deep saucepan over medium heat.

2. Add your cream and bring to a **boil**.

3. As soon as it begins to **boil**, turn down heat and **simmer** for 5 minutes, stirring regularly.

4. **Stir** in the cheese. Add a few shakes of salt and pepper.

5. Let the sauce **cool** and then **pour** it into a jar.

Makes: 1 cup of cocoa mix and 12 spoons

Prep: 20 minutes

You'll need:

125 mL (½ cup) unsweetened cocoa

125 mL (½ cup) sugar

250 mL (1 cup) semi-sweet chocolate chips

12 sturdy plastic spoons

Special equipment:

250 mL (1 cup) glass jar

ribbon

Cocoa and Spoons

Tip Put this on your label!
Mix 25 mL (5 tsp) of cocoa mix with 250 mL (1 cup) hot milk for a steamy treat!

SLURP!

The Mix

1. **Sift** cocoa and sugar together.

2. **Pour** into jar and seal. Attach a label with the instructions above.

The Spoons

1. **Melt** chocolate chips in a bowl over hot, but not boiling, water. Dip each spoon into melted chocolate. Be sure that the bowl of each spoon is completely coated.

Yum.

2. Stand each spoon in a drinking glass (chocolate side up!) and refrigerate for 30 minutes until hardened. Tie spoons to jar with ribbon. Give as a gift with the cocoa mix.

Rocko Chocos

Makes: 12 to 15 large treats, or 20 to 25 little treats

Prep: 25 minutes, plus time to chill

You'll need:

375 mL (1½ cups) semi-sweet chocolate chips

250 mL (1 cup) mini marshmallows

250 mL (1 cup) slivered almonds

80 mL (⅓ cup) white chocolate chips

250 mL (1 cup) crisp rice cereal

1. To **melt** semi-sweet chocolate chips, put in bowl and set over another bowl of hot water. **Stir** until smooth. **Cool** for 10 minutes.

2. **Stir** in remaining ingredients.

3. Line a baking sheet with parchment paper. Drop rounded spoonfuls of mixture onto sheet, about 5 cm (2 in) apart.

4. Place cookie sheet in refrigerator until set. Rocko Chocos can be stored in covered container for about a week, if they last that long!

Stained-Glass Cookies

THESE COOKIES ARE ALMOST TOO BEAUTIFUL TO EAT!

Makes: 2 to 3 dozen cookies

Prep: 1 hour

You'll need:

1 L (4 cups) hard candies, in a variety of colors

500 mL (2 cups) all-purpose flour

2 mL (½ tsp) salt

2 mL (½ tsp) baking powder

125 mL (½ cup) unsalted butter, soft

250 mL (1 cup) sugar

1 egg

5 mL (1 tsp) vanilla

1. **Preheat** oven to 180°C (350°F). Line several cookie sheets with parchment paper. Crush candies of the same color separately by placing in sealed sandwich bags and hitting with a mallet. Put each color in a separate bowl.

crunch crackle

2. **Stir** flour, salt and baking powder together. Set aside. In large bowl, cream butter with sugar until light and fluffy. **Beat** in egg and vanilla. Add flour mixture and **mix** on low speed.

Kitchen Gifts

YEAH, ALMOST!

MUNCH MUNCH

3. Roll dough out to 1/2 cm (1/4 in) thickness on floured surface. Use large cookie cutters to cut shapes, then transfer to the cookie sheets.

4. Use small cookie cutters or a sharp knife to cut shapes out of the middles of unbaked cookies. Fill each hole completely with crushed candies. **Bake** for 7 to 9 minutes, until edges of cookies are golden brown and candies are melted. Gently lift the cookies off the sheets when completely cool.

Tip **Edible Jewelry**
To make stained-glass pendants, make a hole with a straw in the tops of the unbaked cookies!

Index

It's Just What I Wanted!

About the author:
Elisabeth de Mariaffi is a mother of two, freelance writer and poet who loves to cook with kids. Her work for grown-ups has been published across Canada; her work for kids has mainly been seen in her daughter's kindergarten classroom.

For Nora, Desi and Jay who taught me all about cooking with love.

With special thanks to all my amazing recipe-testing kids: Ella and Callum; Melissa, Meghan and Michelle; Madelaine and Heather; Alex, Maddie and Aidan; Shelby, Jade, Mark and Lucas; Stephen and Derek; Lauren and Shannon; Odin; Luke; Soojung and Seungmin.

2nd edition © 2009 Owlkids Books Inc.

Art Direction: Blair Kerrigan/Glyphics and Barb Kelly
Photography: Ian Crysler and Monica McKenna

Consultant: Andrea Olynyk, Registered Dietitian

Special thanks to Abby and Emily Grundy; Helen McGarry; Liza Finlay; Liam Tully and the Owlkids team.

We gratefully acknowledge the financial support of the Government of Canada through the Book Publishing Industry Development Program (BPIDP) for our publishing activities.

 Conseil des Arts   Canada Council
du Canada   for the Arts

Library and Archives Canada Cataloguing in Publication

De Mariaffi, Elisabeth, 1973-
    Eat it up! : lip-smacking recipes for kids / recipes by Elisabeth
    de Mariaffi ; illustrations by Jay Stephens ... [et al.].

Includes index.
"A Chickadee book".
ISBN 978-1-897349-56-4

    1. Cookery--Juvenile literature. I. Title.

TX652.5.D44 2008   j641.5'123   C2008-907580-3

Library of Congress Control Number: 2008941652

Printed in China   JUN 30 2009

Owlkids Books Inc.
10 Lower Spadina Ave., Suite 400
Toronto, Ontario M5V 2Z2
Ph: 416-340-2700
Fax: 416-340-9769

Distributed in Canada by Raincoast Books
905 Shaughnessy Street, Vancouver, British Columbia V6P 6E5

Distributed in the United States by Publishers Group West
1700 Fourth Street, Berkeley, California 94710

 Publisher of chirp chickaDEE **and** OWL

www.owlkids.com